I0796100

Jewish American WOMEN OF ACHIEVEMENT

Naomi Rockler

San Diego, CA

Printed in the United States

For more information, contact:
ReferencePoint Press, Inc.
PO Box 27779
San Diego, CA 92198
www.ReferencePointPress.com

LIBRARY OF CONGRESS CATALOGING-IN-PUBLICATION DATA

Names: Rockler, Naomi author
Title: Jewish American women of achievement / by Naomi Rockler.
Description: San Diego, CA : ReferencePoint Press, Inc, [2026] | Series: Women of achievement | Includes bibliographical references and index.
Identifiers: LCCN 2025002597 (print) | LCCN 2025002598 (ebook) | ISBN 9781678210601 library binding | ISBN 9781678210618 ebook
Subjects: LCSH: Jewish women--United States--Biography--Juvenile literature | Jews--United States--Biography--Juvenile literature | Women--United States--Biography--Juvenile literature | LCGFT: Biographies
Classification: LCC E184.36.W64 R63 2026 (print) | LCC E184.36.W64 (ebook) | DDC 305.48/89240922--dc23/eng/20250320
LC record available at https://lccn.loc.gov/2025002597
LC ebook record available at https://lccn.loc.gov/2025002598

CONTENTS

The Contributions of American Jewish Women

"When I think of strong Jewish women, I think of Ruth Bader Ginsburg and Elena Kagan, who have dedicated their lives to fighting for civil rights on the Supreme Court," explains Sasha Lasakow, a young Jewish woman from Philadelphia. "And then there are the many strong Jewish women who have made a personal impact in my life. . . . There's my grandmother, who worked with the FBI [Federal Bureau of Investigation] in Birmingham, Alabama, in the 1960s to collect insider information on white nationalist groups."[1]

Lasakow's comment is just one way to think about what it means to be a strong, successful Jewish woman in America. Jewish women have been successful in many fields, including business, science, law and politics, literature, and entertainment. Striving to overcome barriers posed by both sexism and anti-Semitism, Jewish women have contributed significantly to American life. "The story of Jewish women in the United States is one of impressive achievement," writes Joyce Antler, a Brandeis University professor. "Despite their numerically small representation in the American population, they made major contributions to politics and culture."[2]

Jewish Women and Business

From colonial times, American Jewish immigrants have made a living by opening businesses. "Through the realm of commerce, Jews made an impression on American life," explains historian Hasia R. Diner. "In most cases their distinctively Jewish last names appeared on the windows and awnings of the stores which lined so many Main Streets and which sprang up in poor and middle-class shopping districts."[3] Some local stores became multimillion-dollar businesses, like Nathan's Famous hot dogs and Bloomingdale's department stores.

> "The story of Jewish women in the United States is one of impressive achievement. Despite their numerically small representation in the American population, they made major contributions to politics and culture."[2]
>
> —Joyce Antler, Brandeis University professor of American Jewish history and culture

Women worked alongside their family members to run family stores and other businesses. Many started their own businesses, sometimes by selling homemade baked goods and hand-sewn clothing. Others were instrumental in building business empires. For example, Regina Margareten—known as the "Matzah Queen of New York" in the early twentieth century—helped turn her family's bakery into a major kosher foods distributor. Another well-known Jewish businesswoman, Ruth Handler, invented the Barbie doll in 1959 and was copresident of Mattel. Prominent American women in business today include Facebook executive Sheryl Sandberg, Oracle chief executive officer Safra Catz, and fashion designer Tory Burch.

Women in Science

Another arena in which Jewish women have been successful is science. As physicist Athene Donald argues in *Not Just for the Boys: Why We Need More Women in Science* (2023), women scientists have had to fight to be taken seriously and get hired. But their intellect and talents have led Jewish women to make significant contributions to the sciences. In 1947 Gerty Cori became the first woman to win the Nobel Prize in Physiology or Medicine for her research on how the body converts sugar into energy. Another scientist, microbiologist Esther Lederberg, developed techniques for studying genetic mutations and antibiotic resistance in the 1950s. Jewish women continue to conduct groundbreaking scientific research today—like environmental scientist Susan Solomon and astrophysicist Andrea Ghez.

Jewish Women in Politics and Law

Jewish women have also made impressive accomplishments in politics and law. American Jewish women have a long tradition of activism, dating back to union organizers like Clara Lemlich and Rose Schneiderman in the late 1800s. Many Jewish women were leaders in the Women's Liberation Movement in the 1970s and 1980s, including Gloria Steinem, Bella Abzug, and Betty Friedan.

Jewish women have also broken barriers by being elected to office. One of the first women to serve in the House of Represen-

Businesswoman Ruth Handler invented the Barbie doll in 1959.

tatives was Jewish—Florence Prag Kahn, who was reelected five times. The first Jewish woman senator, Dianne Feinstein of California, was elected in 1992 and served until her death in 2023. Today's prominent Jewish women politicians include Florida representative Debbie Wasserman Schultz and US secretary of the treasury Janet Yellen.

Jewish women were also pioneers in the legal profession, including Alice Petluck, who became one of the first female lawyers in 1895, and Justine Polier, who in 1935 became the first American woman judge appointed in New York. Of the six women appointed to the Supreme Court, two have been Jewish: Ruth Bader Ginsburg and Elena Kagan.

Women in Entertainment and Literature

American Jewish women have also contributed to entertainment and literature. Throughout the 1800s, Jewish women performed in theater and vaudeville shows. When film arrived, many Jewish women were signed by studios, although many were told to adopt less Jewish-sounding names because of anti-Semitic barriers, sometimes overt and sometimes unspoken. Famous Jewish women in Hollywood included Lauren Bacall, Hedy Lamarr, and Lillian Roth. Television also featured Jewish women, including Gertrude Berg of *The Goldbergs* (1949–1956), a popular show about a Jewish family. Today, well-known Jewish actresses include Natalie Portman, Scarlett Johansson, and Rashida Jones.

Jewish women have also been prominent in literature. Some have written about Jewish themes, like contemporary novelist Nicole Krauss. Others have written in many genres, like science-fiction writer Marge Piercy, women's fiction writer Jennifer Weiner, and mystery novelist Faye Kellerman.

Jewish American women have made remarkable strides across diverse fields, overcoming both sexism and anti-Semitism. Their contributions reflect a legacy of resilience and leadership, inspiring future generations to pursue excellence.

CHAPTER ONE

Ida Cohen Rosenthal, Businesswoman

After World War II ended in 1945, many women were pressured to get married, have children, and abandon any career aspirations they may have. While some women were happy in these traditional roles, others dreamed of careers and other possibilities. These dreams were once portrayed in an unlikely venue—an ad campaign for Maidenform bras.

> "Customers could spirit themselves away from the doldrums of domestic life and into the imaginary world of Maidenform, where a woman could be and do anything she wanted."[4]
>
> —Sierra B. Holt, fashion historian

Before 1949 most undergarment advertisements featured modest illustrations of women wearing these products; they rarely featured actual models. Maidenform's I Dreamed campaign changed this approach. These ads—which ran for two decades starting in 1949—used live models wearing nothing above the waist but a Maidenform bra. The unusual aspect of each advertisement was that the models were often role-playing activities associated with male-dominated professions. The taglines included statements like "I dreamed I was a fireman in my Maidenform bra" or "I dreamed I won the election in my Maidenform bra." Other Maidenform-clad women in the ads dreamed of going back to school, serving on a jury, or playing in a symphony.

In women's magazines, the I Dreamed ads stood out from the typical ads aimed at women, which almost exclusively depicted housewives in domestic roles. As fashion historian Sierra B. Holt states, "From these advertisements, customers could spirit themselves away from the doldrums of domestic life and into the imaginary world of Maidenform, where a woman could be and do anything she wanted."[4]

Appropriately, the marketing mastermind who dreamed up this ad campaign was an outspoken and unconventional career woman—Ida Cohen Rosenthal. In the 1920s Rosenthal helped design the modern bra and then cofounded Maidenform, one of the most successful bra manufacturers in the world. "Always

The I Dreamed ad campaign for Maidenform bras was invented by the marketing mastermind Ida Cohen Rosenthal.

independent and willing to take chances, Ida Cohen Rosenthal was a business leader at a time when women were not easily accepted in leadership roles,"[5] wrote Joy A. Kingsolver of the Jewish Women's Archive.

Early Life and Work

Ida Cohen Rosenthal was born Ida Kaganovich in 1886 in a small Russian village called Rakov. Life was hard for eastern European Jews at this time. Because of anti-Semitism that unfairly painted Jews as an inferior race bent on global economic domination, Russian Jews were forced to live in a crowded geographic region on the western border. Known as the Pale, there they struggled with poverty and the threat of violence from nationalist or majority groups.

For most Jewish girls at the time, work outside the home after marriage was not a possibility; tradition dictated that they marry young, often in unions arranged by a matchmaker. However, Rosenthal's childhood home was unusual. Her father was a scholar who studied the Torah and the Talmud (Jewish religious texts). This was a position of honor in the community—and an unpaid one. Because her father did not earn a salary, Rosenthal's mother was the family breadwinner and managed a general store, which normalized the idea for her that women could work outside the home. She also learned from her mother the value of hard work and responsibility, since she was the oldest child of seven and worked alongside her mother to manage the household, the family livestock, and the store.

As a teenager, Rosenthal and her sister Ettel became dressmaking apprentices to a local seamstress. Once the apprenticeship was over, their mother purchased a sewing machine for them, hoping that this would give them more financial independence than most women in town. The sisters started a successful home dressmaking business. To expand their customer base, Rosenthal traveled to the nearby city of Minsk to sell dresses—an unusual thing for a young girl from the country to do at the time.

Pigeon Vests and World War II

Like many companies during World War II, Maidenform turned its manufacturing facilities over to the military to make products needed for the war effort. Although Maidenform's facilities did continue to produce bras—primarily for members of the Women's Army Corps—Maidenform's greatest contribution to the war was the manufacture of about twenty-eight thousand vests for carrier pigeons.

Carrier pigeons were an essential part of the war effort. They were trained to deliver messages, which were attached to their legs inside canisters. After the pigeons were equipped with the canisters, paratroopers parachuted into enemy territory with the pigeons, which were released after the paratrooper landed on the ground. The birds then flew back to Allied lines. To secure their safety during the jump, the pigeons wore tightly woven vests that were specially shaped for their bodies. The vests had a strap that was used to connect the pigeon securely to the paratrooper's jacket. Carrier pigeon vests may seem like a very different product than a bra. However, they are made of similar materials, and both contraptions have a sling-like construction, so it made sense for a factory that produced bras to switch to pigeon vests.

At age seventeen, she further defied tradition by going to work in a factory in Warsaw and by enrolling in a secondary school to study math and Russian literature.

Political Activism

As an outspoken young woman, political activism was a natural fit for Rosenthal, even though such a thing was dangerous in what was then part of the Russian Empire under Tsar Nicholas II. In Warsaw she became involved with the Jewish Labor Bund, a political movement that sought to end anti-Semitism and fight for socialism in Russia and the end of the tsarist regime. After returning to Rakov, Rosenthal became a leader in the local bund organization. She became outright rebellious, openly smoking cigarettes and learning how to use weapons in case the community was targeted by anti-Semites.

During this time, she fell in love with William "Wolf" Rosenthal, a quiet artist who was also a bund member. The couple's courtship was interrupted by misfortune when William's brother and sister-in-law were arrested for their bundist activities. Then, as the Russo-Japanese War began, William was conscripted into the Russian army—a death sentence for the majority of conscripted Jews, who were given inadequate training and equipment, along with the most dangerous combat positions. William devised a plan to bribe the guards and escape into the woods, where Ida had stored his street clothes. Alone, William then left for America.

Ida stayed in Rakov in part because of the Russian Revolution that began in 1905. She wanted to fight on behalf of the rebellion. Then a local police officer warned her mother that if she did not stop, she would be imprisoned—which, like conscription, often meant death for a bundist Jew. When she was nineteen, Rosenthal's parents persuaded her to emigrate to America for her safety. They hoped their family members in Hoboken, New Jersey, would keep an eye on her and encourage her to live a more traditional life.

Setting Up Business

Rosenthal agreed to go, but she was not set on becoming a traditional homemaker. Her American family encouraged her to use her sewing skills to get a job in a factory and then get married and settle down. Instead, Rosenthal went into business for herself. Adamant about not working for someone else, she bought a sewing machine on an installment plan and started making dresses at home. She later wrote, "If you really want to make it, become an entrepreneur. Then you are in charge of your own destiny."[6] Although she could barely speak English, she carefully studied women's magazines to make sure her designs matched the current fashion trends.

> "If you really want to make it, become an entrepreneur. Then you are in charge of your own destiny."[6]
>
> —Ida Cohen Rosenthal

Rosenthal reconnected with William, and they married in 1906. Bucking another tradition, she chose not to wear a modest Orthodox Jewish wedding dress and instead sewed her own gown that hit above the ankle—a daring statement in 1906. On their honeymoon, William became very ill, and although he recovered, it was clear that he was not strong enough to be the primary breadwinner. Having grown up with a working mother, and with years of working experience, Rosenthal was up to the challenge. The couple eventually had two children, Louis in 1907 and Beatrice in 1916. Throughout their marriage, William was the primary caretaker of the children.

Rosenthal set up her own dressmaking shop in Hoboken, and her business flourished. In 1912 she employed six seamstresses. Her dresses sold for as much as $7.50 apiece, which was the equivalent of over $200 in 2024. Capitalizing on her success, she moved her business to Manhattan, where she could sell dresses to wealthier clients for three times as much. Then in 1921 a prestigious dressmaker named Enid Bisset noticed one of her customers wearing a Rosenthal dress. Bisset was so impressed that she invited Rosenthal to go into business with her. They opened a posh store together called Enid's Frocks.

The New Bra

Reflecting the flapper fashion of the 1920s, many of the dresses at Enid's Frocks had straight, loose-fitting silhouettes that hung from the shoulders with minimal emphasis on a woman's curves or her waistline. This style flattered women who had straight, boyish figures, but it was not flattering for women with curvaceous bodies and larger breasts. This was especially frustrating for Rosenthal, who was a large and curvaceous woman.

The problem was made worse because of the lack of supportive undergarments. In past years women had worn corsets—restrictive garments designed to give women's bodies an hourglass shape. Corsets, which were often painful to wear, had fallen out of fashion and had been replaced with the first bras. These strapless, bandeau-style bras were designed to bind women's breasts. They were uncomfortable and constrained breathing, and for women with larger breasts, the tightness made cleavage disappear, creating an unflattering look.

Some customers complained about how the store's dresses did not fit various body shapes. Faced with the criticism, Rosenthal and Bisset experimented with ways to make their dresses more accommodating. They decided the best way to solve the problem was to create a better bra for women to wear under their dresses. They modified a bandeau-style bra so that it had separate cups of fabric for each breast. Combined with the use of straps and an elastic band, the modified bra lifted and separated the breasts and raised them away from the body, which was much more comfortable while still being supportive. Ida consulted William, and he used his artistic skills to improve on their prototype. His design used satin to make the straps prettier and a three-hook strap for attaching the bra securely in the back.

At first, Rosenthal and Bisset simply gave the bras away to customers when they purchased a dress. Sometimes they sewed the bras inside the dresses. Yet something happened that they did not expect. Women loved the bras so much that they came to the shop just to buy them. Rosenthal and Bisset started manufacturing as many bras as they could in their shop, selling premade bras for a dollar and custom-made bras for up to fifty dollars apiece—the equivalent of over $800 in today's dollars. Word spread throughout the city, and business exploded. "No one had heard of a brassiere in 1920," wrote journalist David Laskin. "By 1924, all the fashionable women had to have one."[7]

"Nature made women with a bosom, so why fight nature?"[8]

—Ida Cohen Rosenthal

In 1925 Rosenthal and Bisset gave up their dressmaking business to exclusively manufacture and market their new product. They opened a manufacturing facility in Bayonne, New Jersey, and hired a salesman to sell bras to department stores. By the end of the decade, they were manufacturing over five hundred thousand bras a year. They chose the name Maiden Form (later changed to Maidenform) for their new company to highlight the fact that

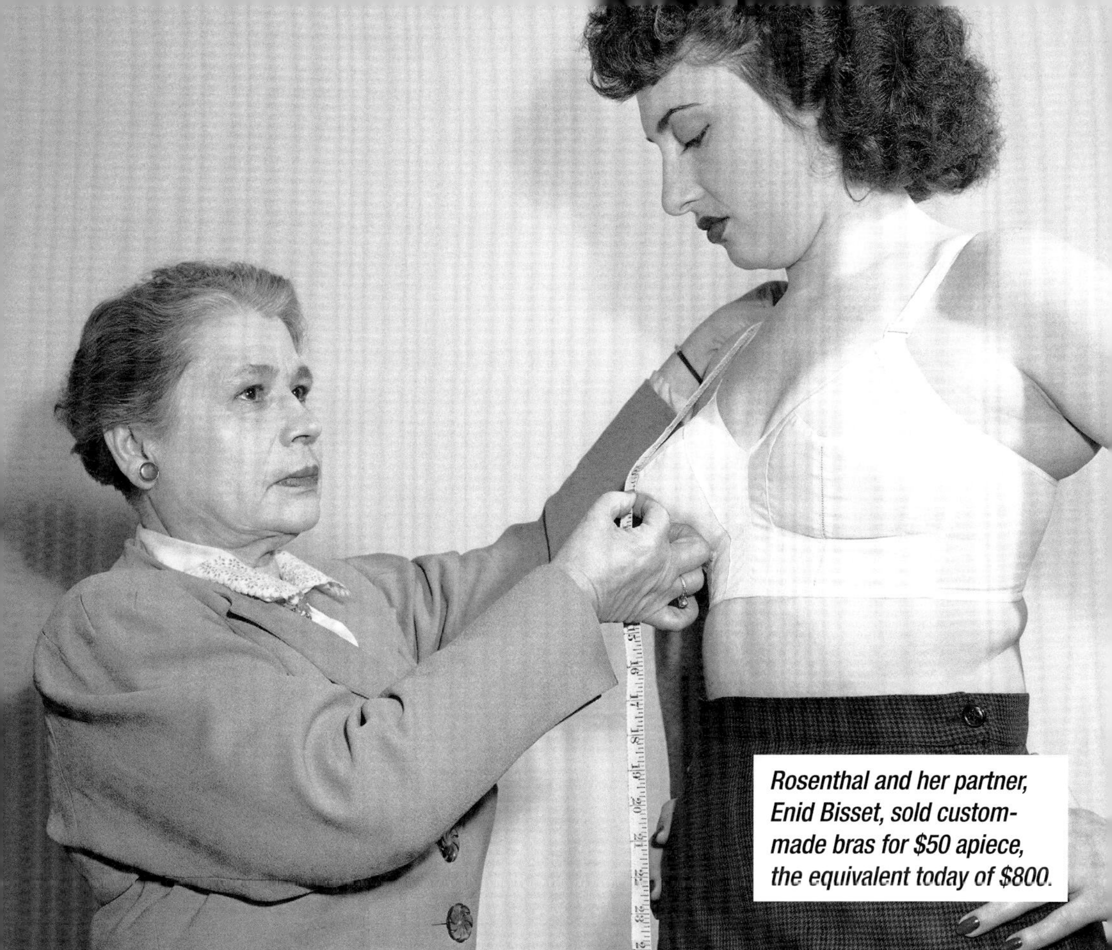

Rosenthal and her partner, Enid Bisset, sold custom-made bras for $50 apiece, the equivalent today of $800.

unlike boyish bandeau-style bras, their bras highlighted and enhanced the female form. "Nature made women with a bosom," argued Rosenthal, "so why fight nature?"[8]

Maidenform

Bisset retired from the business in the 1930s due to illness. Under the direction of the Rosenthals, Maidenform became one of the most successful bra manufacturers in the world. The company's success was largely due to the couple's drive to continuously innovate. They updated the bra with design innovations that are standard today, including adjustable straps and a more secure attachment system, and they created maternity and nursing bras. In addition, they developed the cup-size system for measuring bra size that became a standard throughout the industry.

A Family Legacy

Ida Cohen Rosenthal learned from her mother that women belonged in the workplace—and she passed this along to her daughter, Beatrice Rosenthal Coleman. After Beatrice graduated from Barnard College in 1938, her mother asked her to join the company. Beatrice had studied to become a teacher but jumped at the opportunity to follow in her mother's footsteps. "When my mother asked me to come into the business, I was overjoyed," she said. "I'd always admired my mother. She was an entrepreneur at a time when entrepreneurial women were few and far between." Rosenthal insisted that her daughter learn the company from the ground up and put her to work initially on the production line. Eventually, she worked for the advertising department, and in 1968 she became president of the company. Later, Ida Cohen Rosenthal's granddaughter, Elizabeth Coleman, also rose to an executive position at Maidenform. She served as the chief executive officer of the company for several years during the 1990s.

Quoted in *Entrepreneur*, "Enid Bisset, Ida Rosenthal & William Rosenthal," October 10, 2008. www.entrepreneur.com.

As part of their innovative spirit, the Rosenthals developed new products to keep up with cultural trends. For example, they capitalized on Hollywood's popularization of busty silhouettes in the 1950s by creating a bra that dramatically accentuated the bust. Better known as the "bullet bra," the Chansonette featured a cone-shaped silhouette with prominent points at the nipples. The bullet bra became one of the most iconic clothing staples of the 1950s and 1960s. At the same time, Maidenform's marketing strategy included building brand loyalty by selling its older products alongside its innovative new ones.

Although William was the president of Maidenform, he and his wife ran the company as equals. He oversaw design and production. She handled the financial side of the business, including negotiations with unions, and collaborated with factory workers to create a more efficient production system for manufacturing bras. Rosenthal was also very adept at advertising and public relations, including her wildly successful I Dreamed advertising campaign. She intentionally marketed herself as the face of Maidenform, using her personal immigrant-makes-good story of success to appeal to the public. When William died in 1958, she became the president of Maidenform—an extremely unusual position for a woman to hold in the 1950s.

Ida Cohen Rosenberg died of pneumonia in 1973 at age eighty-seven. In 2013—nearly a century after it was founded—Maidenform was acquired by Hanesbrands for $583 million. Maidenform continues to manufacture bras. The outspoken woman who refused to conform to traditional gender roles made a permanent impact on how women dress and live. "Through Ida's efforts, Maidenform brought comfort and security to women's wardrobes," writes Sierra B. Holt. "A Maidenform garment allowed the wearer to embrace the fashionable silhouettes of any given era: the 1920s Flapper, the 1930s Hollywood Siren, or the New Look of the 1940s and 1950s, without forgetting the practical bends, snaps, and turns of everyday life. Women could work and live in their Maidenform."[9]

Gertrude Elion, Biochemist and Pharmacologist

In 1933 fifteen-year-old Gertrude Elion was very close to her grandfather, a Russian Jewish immigrant who was a watchmaker and a scholar. He and his granddaughter took walks together, speaking Yiddish and telling each other stories.

Then Elion's grandfather got stomach cancer, for which there was no treatment at the time. When she visited him at the hospital, she was horrified to witness his excruciating final months. Elion, who was graduating from high school, decided on a future path. "I already knew from my high school courses that I loved science," she wrote, "but that year I was so devastated from my grandfather's death from cancer that majoring in Chemistry seemed like the logical first step in committing myself to fight the disease."[10]

Elion followed through with her decision to fight cancer—and that was just one of her accomplishments. In addition to helping design one of the first drugs to treat childhood leukemia, Elion developed drugs to fight gout, lupus, rheumatoid arthritis, and organ transplant rejection. Her pioneering work on antiviral drugs led to treatments for chicken pox, herpes, shingles, and human immunodeficiency virus (HIV). In 1988 Elion won the Nobel Prize—the world's highest scientific honor—for her work in medicine.

But Elion did more than just discover cures and treatments for specific conditions; she pioneered research methods that changed the way that pathologists investigate diseases in general. As the Nobel Prize's official website explains, "Simply put, Elion changed the way researchers develop drugs. As a result, although she died in 1999 at the age of 81, Gertrude Elion is still saving lives."[11]

Early Life

When they were teenagers, Elion's parents emigrated from eastern Europe with their families. They reached the United States and settled in the Bronx—a borough of New York City—where Elion was born in 1918. Elion's father worked as a dentist, and her mother was a homemaker who made extra money as a seamstress. Her younger brother Herbert was born in 1923; he would also go on to have a celebrated career in the sciences.

Elion's parents were very frugal and taught their children the value of hard work. Even though it was unusual for women to have a career at the time, Elion's parents strongly encouraged her to do so. "I think perhaps it was my mother who influenced me the most," wrote Elion. "She was a housewife. She had no higher education, but had the most common sense of anyone I knew, and she wanted me to have a career."[12] Elion was a voracious reader from a young age and loved books about scientists, including Marie Curie, the first woman ever to win a Nobel Prize.

Elion's hardworking father lost all his money during the stock market crash of 1929, but because of her excellent high school grades, she was able to attend Hunter College free of tuition. Hunter was a women's college at the time, with a largely male faculty who prepared female students to become teachers. Elion was lucky to have a male chemistry teacher who took female students seriously and set up a study group for them to discuss recent scientific discoveries. Elion graduated near the top of her class in 1937 when she was only nineteen. Although most of the chemistry majors in her class went on to be nurses or teachers, she was determined to become a scientist, largely due to her motivation to help cancer patients like her grandfather.

Gertrude Elion loved books about famous scientists like Marie Curie (pictured), the first woman ever to win a Nobel Prize.

Struggles

Despite Elion's stellar grades and her drive to succeed, it was nearly impossible for a woman in the 1930s to break into the field of chemistry. She applied to fifteen graduate schools and was not accepted into any of them. She was also unable to get a job at a laboratory. Jobs were scarce because of the Great Depression, and as a woman, it was unlikely that she would be hired over a man. At one interview, Elion was told the laboratory could not hire her because she was too pretty and would distract male coworkers. "Nobody took me seriously," wrote Elion. "They wondered why in the world I wanted to be a chemist when no women were doing that. The world was not waiting for me."[13]

Elion was determined not to give up her dream. With the goal of eventually attending graduate school, she did what she could to earn money. She attended secretarial school and taught chemistry to nurses and high school students. She was finally accepted to

New York University to earn a master's degree in chemistry, which she paid for from the money she had saved from working.

> "Nobody took me seriously. They wondered why in the world I wanted to be a chemist when no women were doing that."[13]
>
> —Gertrude Elion

While she was in graduate school, Elion started dating a brilliant statistician named Leonard Canter. They dated for four years, sending each other love letters from across town, and planned to marry. "In you I find most of what others must find in religion," she wrote, "faith, hope, consolation, beauty, ecstasy of an almost unearthly quality, and a deep transcending love."[14] Despite the rigid gender norms of the era, Canter did not expect Elion to give up her career after marriage. But tragically, Canter developed an infection of the heart—which could have been treatable with antibiotics if he had gotten sick five years later. After months of illness, he died in 1941 with Elion by his side. She was devastated and was more determined than ever to become a scientist so she could find cures for diseases. She never married.

Elion was finally able to get a job working at a chemistry lab after World War II started. With so many men fighting overseas, jobs in scientific fields opened to women to fill the labor shortage.

Elion as Teacher and Mentor

In addition to her drug innovations, Gertrude Elion was very proud of her work as a teaching professor and as a mentor of medical students. She taught classes as an adjunct professor at Duke University from 1971 until 1983. Then, after officially retiring, she became a research professor until her death in 1999. Elion was a mentor to third-year medical students and graduate students, publishing over twenty-five papers with students over the years. Students may have been flustered at first to work with someone so famous, but she had a knack for putting them at ease and for making herself very available to answer questions. She valued sharing her love of research with a new generation. Her legacy continues with several academic awards, including the Gertrude B. Elion Mentored Medical Student Research Award, an award for female medical students pursuing health-related research at the Duke University School of Medicine and the University of North Carolina School of Medicine.

She was hired as a food chemist at a lab in New York, where she tested things like the color of egg yolks and the acidity of pickles. Although she appreciated the opportunity to work in a laboratory environment, she did not feel intellectually stimulated.

A Groundbreaking Career at Burroughs Wellcome

Elion finally got her big break in 1944, when she was hired by pharmaceutical company Burroughs Wellcome as an assistant biochemist. Unlike many pharmaceutical companies, which were motivated by profits, Burroughs Wellcome had a reputation for hiring research scientists dedicated to finding cures for serious illnesses.

Elion stayed at Burroughs Wellcome for thirty-nine years, working closely with prominent researcher George Hitchings. Together, Elion and Hitchings revolutionized the way that scientists developed drugs. At the time, most drug research was done by using a trial-and-error method until effective treatments were

Testing the color of egg yolks was one of Elion's jobs in the lab where she was hired as a food chemist.

found. Instead, Elion and Hitchings developed a method called rational drug design. With this approach, the pair targeted specific cellular elements—such as proteins or enzymes—associated with a disease process. Physicians could then inject compounds that bind with these elements and inhibit their role in the process, thus suppressing or eradicating the disease. This method saved time and lives because it led more quickly to effective treatments.

Treating Cancer

In 1950 rational drug design led Elion to one of her most important breakthroughs: a drug called 6-mercaptopurine, which treats leukemia by interfering with the development of cancerous cells. This was one of the first drugs to effectively treat cancer, a goal that had been important to her since her grandfather had died of stomach cancer years before.

> **"Research is very hard work. How you handle the setbacks can make a difference. You must never feel you have failed."[15]**
>
> **—Gertrude Elion**

Elion and Hitchings worked closely with patients who were taking the drug, getting to know them personally in a way that was not typical of pharmaceutical researchers. Many of the patients were children who had been diagnosed with childhood leukemia. Elion felt a strong emotional investment in her patients; she felt joy when they went into remission and sorrow when the disease overcame the treatment and the patients died. Elion was especially distraught when a young woman patient to whom she had become close died; the woman got married and had a child after she seemed to be cured of cancer, but the cancer came back. Setbacks like this inspired Elion to work harder to develop more effective drugs. "Research is very hard work," she wrote. "How you handle the setbacks can make a difference. You must never feel you have failed. You can always come back to something later, when you have more knowledge or better equipment, and try again."[15]

Elion transformed the way cancer is treated. Today, 6-mercaptopurine remains a key component of cancer treatment, particularly in treating childhood leukemia. Before the development of this drug, children diagnosed with leukemia typically lived only a few months. Today the survival rate for children diagnosed with leukemia before age fourteen is over 90 percent.

In addition to fighting cancer, 6-mercaptopurine contributed to a breakthrough in organ transplantation. In the 1950s attempts to transplant healthy organs into sick patients were unsuccessful because the human body's immune system recognizes new organs as foreign objects and rejects them. To solve this problem, Elion developed a variation of her cancer drug, azathioprine, that suppressed the immune system's response to new organs. This made transplantation possible. Later, azathioprine was used to treat autoimmune disorders like lupus and rheumatoid arthritis.

Antiviral Drugs

One of Elion's most significant breakthroughs was the development of an antiviral drug that was approved in 1977. Before this time, antiviral drugs were widely considered to be an impossible fantasy. As the Nobel Prize website explains, "Scientists doubted that drugs could be invented to fight viruses; any substance that would kill a virus would be too toxic for the body to endure."[16] To get around this, Elion developed acyclovir, a drug that does not kill viruses but instead stops them from spreading so that the immune system has more time to fight the virus.

Initially, acyclovir was used to fight herpes, Epstein-Barr, chicken pox, and shingles. Its innovative approach led to the development of many other antiviral drugs. After she retired, Elion continued to work with her old research team to develop the antiviral drug AZT, the first successful drug used to fight the HIV virus that causes acquired immunodeficiency syndrome (AIDS). Antiviral drugs have since been developed to fight hepatitis, Ebola, influenza (the flu), and respiratory syncytial virus, a virus that can be fatal for infants. Most recently, many COVID-19 patients who are at risk for serious infections are prescribed Paxlovid, a powerful antiviral medication.

Elion's Family

After Gertrude Elion's fiancé died when she was twenty-three years old, she did not have any serious romantic relationships. While some of this was because she was heartbroken over the loss of the man she loved, it was also because of the stigma of being both a married woman and a working woman, especially in male-dominated scientific fields. "This was a time when women couldn't have both a family and a career very easily," she wrote. "In those days it would have been very much frowned on for a married woman to be working, or to come back to the lab if she had a child."

Although she did not have children of her own, Elion was very close to her younger brother Herbert's children and grandchildren. When she won the Nobel Prize in 1988, she brought eleven family members to the ceremony in Sweden with her, including four children under age five. Elion insisted that the young children be allowed to attend the formal banquet, saying that she was not going to bring them all to Sweden just to have them stay in a hotel room. It turned out that the children were well behaved.

Quoted in Catherine Whitlock and Rhodri Evans, *10 Women Who Changed Science and the World*. New York: Diversion, 2019, p. 85.

The impact of acyclovir and other antiviral drugs has been revolutionary. Although antiviral drugs are not a cure, they can dramatically reduce the risk of serious side effects from dangerous infections. For example, antiviral drugs used to treat chicken pox reduce the risk of more serious infections like pneumonia. Thanks to antiviral treatments for HIV, patients can live indefinitely without developing AIDS, a disease that killed millions of people before antivirals were developed. Moreover, antiviral drugs serve an important public health function. Because they reduce the amount of time that people are sick with dangerous infections, antiviral medications help reduce the transmission rate of these infections.

The Nobel Prize and Elion's Legacy

In 1988 Elion—along with Hitchings and fellow researcher James W. Black—was awarded the Nobel Prize in Physiology or Medicine. Elion was only the fifth woman to receive the Nobel Prize in this category since it was first awarded in 1908, and only the second Jewish woman. The prize was awarded not for a specific drug but for the development of many, along with their role in the transformation of how drugs are researched. A colleague of Elion explained, "In awarding them the Nobel, the prize committee said that their work was so important that each of the drugs for which they were honored could have won the prize in itself. . . . This record of drug discovery is unlikely ever to be equaled."[17]

Elion, who was seventy years old when she received the Nobel Prize, did not get overly excited about this high honor. To

At the age of seventy, Elion won the Nobel Prize in Physiology or Medicine. To Elion, the real prize was knowing that she had helped people.

her, the greater prize was knowing that she had helped people. "What we were aiming at was getting people well, and the satisfaction of that is much greater than any prize you can get,"[18] she wrote.

> **"What we were aiming at was getting people well, and the satisfaction of that is much greater than any prize you can get."[18]**
>
> **—Gertrude Elion**

Elion kept a file of letters from patients and their families, thanking her for creating drugs that had saved or extended their lives. She especially treasured the letters she received from children who were living with leukemia. One of the letters she read most was from a patient who had taken Zorivax, a drug she developed to treat shingles. The letter said, "After a very severe case of shingles, Zorivax saved my eyesight. If you ever feel unappreciated for any reason, please take out this letter and reread it."[19]

Gertrude Elion died in 1999 of a cerebral hemorrhage. She was eighty-one years old. Despite the obstacles she faced as a female chemist in an era when such a thing was rare, Elion went on to become one of the most impactful pharmacological researchers in history. The drugs that she developed—and the methods she used for developing them—have saved millions of lives.

CHAPTER THREE

Ruth Bader Ginsburg, Supreme Court Justice

It is not common that an eighty-year-old woman becomes a pop culture icon and a hero to young people, but that is what happened to Supreme Court justice Ruth Bader Ginsburg in 2013. Law student Shana Knizhnik started a Tumblr called "Notorious RBG"—a play on the similarity between Ginsburg's initials and those of the rapper Notorious B.I.G. The moniker spread, and soon the image of Ginsburg in her frilly lace collar appeared on T-shirts, posters, tote bags, and other merchandise. There were Notorious RBG memes and action figures, RBG Halloween costumes, and skits on *Saturday Night Live*, in which Ginsburg was impersonated by comedian Kate McKinnon. Ginsburg embraced this surprising development. "It was beyond my wildest imagination that I would one day become the Notorious RBG,"[20] she said.

The outpouring of appreciation and affection for Ginsburg derived from her career-long advocacy for women's equality, reproductive rights, and social justice. After her death in 2020, people across the country mourned her loss because she had inspired them personally. "RBG was one of my inspirations in coming to law school," explained Rachel Samuels, a Boston University law school student. "As a Jewish woman, seeing her success and tireless advocacy was a constant source of strength and hope that I could do the same. If I could have even a fraction of the impact she had on our country, I would be so proud."[21]

Early Life

Ruth Bader Ginsburg (birth name Joan Ruth Bader) was born in Brooklyn, New York, on March 15, 1933. Her father, Nathan, was a Jewish immigrant from Odessa, Ukraine, and her mother, Celia, was the daughter of Polish Jewish immigrants. Ginsburg was only a year old when her sister, Marilyn, died of meningitis, so she was raised as an only child.

"In those ancient days, most parents of girls wanted them to find Prince Charming and live happily ever after. But my mother wanted me to fend for myself."[22]

—Ruth Bader Ginsburg

As a child, Ginsburg's mother had loved school, but her parents chose to send her brother to college and not her. She was expected to help pay for her brother's Cornell University education by working in a garment factory. Because of this apparent injustice, Ginsburg's mother was determined to send her daughter to college and teach her to be independent. "In those ancient days, most parents of girls wanted them to find Prince Charming and live happily ever after," recalled Ginsburg. "But my mother wanted me to fend for myself."[22]

The image of Ruth Bader Ginsburg in her frilly lace collar appeared on merchandise such as these action figures.

Judaism was an important part of Ginsburg's childhood, but it was also where she first experienced gender discrimination. When her male cousin was thirteen, he had a bar mitzvah, a Jewish coming-of-age ceremony at which a boy reads from the Torah. Ginsburg was jealous because as a girl, she was not allowed to have a bat mitzvah—the equivalent ceremony for girls—because celebrating a girl's coming of age was rare even within Jewish circles in 1946. Then, when Ginsburg's mother died the day before Ruth's high school graduation, she was angered when she was not allowed to be part of the minyan, an official group of male mourners within the community who are selected to pray ceremonially. "She was extremely indignant about it," says Jane Sherron De Hart, author of a biography about Ginsburg. "She felt it was an affront to her mother, and there was nothing she could do about it."[23]

Ginsburg Chooses a Law Career

Per her mother's wishes, Ginsburg enrolled at Cornell in 1950. She did not consider going into law at first, because there were so few women in that profession. But several factors led Ginsburg to consider law. One was her experience with anti-Semitism. As a teenager, she was horrified by the news of the murder of 6 million European Jews in the Holocaust. When her family traveled in America, she saw hotels with signs like "No dogs or Jews." In high school she knew she had to work extra hard because colleges had quotas that restricted the number of Jewish applicants. At Cornell, Jewish students lived in a separate dorm to limit other students' contact with them. These experiences inspired Ginsburg to fight for justice—a value she saw as an integral part of Jewish tradition. "The demand for justice runs through the entirety of the Jewish tradition,"[24] she wrote.

> **"The demand for justice runs through the entirety of the Jewish tradition."[24]**
>
> **—Ruth Bader Ginsburg**

At Cornell, Ginsburg's decision to go into law was also influenced by the "red scare" of the early 1950s. During this fear-

Ginsburg and her husband, Martin, were married for fifty-six years.

ful time, Senator Joseph McCarthy of Wisconsin led aggressive Senate hearings in which citizens who had expressed left-wing views were accused of being Communists and anti-American. Even if untrue, the stigma of affiliation with communism during the Cold War meant that many who were brought before the Senate were blacklisted within their professions. Several lost friends and could not find work. Ginsburg watched this unjust persecution with horror. But she noted that the defendants' lawyers were speaking up for their clients' free speech rights, and this championing of fundamental American liberties inspired Ginsburg to go into law herself.

Ginsburg's husband, Martin, whom she met at Cornell and married in 1954, encouraged her to follow her interest. "He was the only boy I ever met who cared that I had a brain,"[25] she said. Unlike many men at the time, Ginsburg did not expect his wife to

Ruth Bader Ginsburg's Female Role Models

As a girl, Ginsburg considered her mother to be her most important role model. But she had other strong female role models as well. One of them was fictitious—Nancy Drew, the lead character of a series of teen mystery novels first published in 1930. For Ginsburg, Nancy stood out because in most books for young people, the girl characters were passive while the boys were active. "Nancy Drew was a doer," recalled Ginsburg. "She was leading around her boyfriend. She had adventures. She solved mysteries." Another role model of Ginsburg's was Amelia Earhart, the pioneering American aviator who was the first female pilot to fly solo across the Atlantic Ocean. Ginsburg also admired Anne Frank, the teenage girl who hid with her family from the Nazis during the Holocaust and wrote about her experiences in her diary. In her speeches, Ginsburg often quoted a passage of Frank's diary that talked about how she was fed up with the notion that women were inferior to men.

Quoted in Melville House, ed., *Ruth Bader Ginsburg: The Last Interview*. New York: Melville House, 2020, p. 162.

be a homemaker, even after she gave birth to their daughter, Jane, in 1955 and their son, James, in 1965. They were equals in their fifty-six-year marriage, with Martin doing the cooking because his wife was terrible at it. Ginsburg's equal marriage inspired her to fight against gender inequality in the law because she saw firsthand that oppressive gender roles did not have to be the norm.

Struggles

Ginsburg's Notorious RBG moniker fit in part because she was tough. Throughout her life, she overcame both personal and professional obstacles. "Profound challenges—the loss of her mother the day before she graduated from high school, her husband's struggle with cancer while they were both in law school—fueled her fierce determination to accomplish her dreams and achieve justice for others,"[26] argues Tomiko Brown-Nagin, a Harvard Law School professor.

In addition to these personal difficulties, Ginsburg faced challenges in her law career because of gender discrimination. When she began Harvard Law School in 1956, she was one of only nine women in a class of over five hundred. Many professors and male students were hostile toward the women. The dean invited the women to his home for dinner, where he made each of them stand and justify why they were taking a space at Harvard that could have gone to a man.

Despite these obstacles, Ginsburg excelled in her classes and was the first woman to serve on the *Harvard Law Review*, the prestigious journal of legal scholarship. When her husband, also a Harvard law student, nearly died of cancer, Ginsburg attended his classes, took notes, and managed her own coursework while raising a young child. Ginsburg eventually transferred to Columbia Law School and graduated as valedictorian.

Despite outstanding recommendations from professors, Ginsburg struggled to find a job because many law firms refused to hire women lawyers. She was rejected by thirteen firms before finally being offered a position in 1959 as a clerk under a US district judge. When this ended after two years, she was offered jobs at law firms but always at a much lower salary than male applicants. She searched for an academic job in 1963, but similarly, prestigious law schools refused to hire women. She ultimately acquired a position teaching at Rutgers Law School. Even there, the dean informed her she would be paid less because her husband had a good job. When she became pregnant, she wore baggy clothes to hide her pregnancy, lest she lose her job or the respect of her colleagues. In 1972 she was finally hired by Columbia Law School, where she became the first woman to receive tenure.

Fighting for Equality

These experiences fueled Ginsburg's interest in fighting against gender inequality and other forms of discrimination. She saw her role as largely educational. "As an advocate in gender discrimination cases in the seventies, I thought of myself as akin to a grade school teacher," she recalled. "The idea was to educate . . . to help [people] comprehend what it is like, what life is like for people who are different."[27]

Ginsburg established her reputation for fighting against gender discrimination in the 1972 case *Moritz v. Commissioner of Internal Revenue*. She and her husband, who was then a tax attorney, represented Charles Moritz, an unmarried man who had been denied a common tax deduction for being a caregiver to his mother. The Internal Revenue Service said that only women and married men were eligible. The US Court of Appeals ruled in Moritz's favor.

> **"As an advocate in gender discrimination cases in the seventies, I thought of myself as akin to a grade school teacher. The idea was to educate."[27]**
>
> **—Ruth Bader Ginsburg**

Many of the cases Ginsburg argued stemmed from her involvement with the American Civil Liberties Union, through which she cofounded the Women's Rights Project in 1971. She argued several cases before the Supreme Court, including *Reed v. Reed* (1971). In this case Ginsburg challenged an Idaho law that automatically preferred men over women as administrators of estates. This proved to be a landmark decision because it was the first time the court used the equal protection clause of the Fourteenth Amendment to overturn a law that discriminated against women. Other cases she argued included *Weinberger v. Wiesenfeld* (1975), which ruled in favor of a widower who was denied Social Security survivor benefits because he was a man, and *Frontiero v. Richardson* (1973), which gave women in the US military equal benefits policies.

In 1980 Ginsburg was appointed to the US Court of Appeals for the District of Columbia Circuit by President Jimmy Carter. She earned a reputation for being a consensus builder, working well with colleagues who were more conservative than she was.

The Supreme Court

In 1993 President Bill Clinton nominated Ginsburg as an associate justice of the Supreme Court, and the Senate confirmed

Ginsburg was the first Jewish woman to serve on the Supreme Court.

her nomination almost unanimously. Over her twenty-seven-year tenure, Ginsburg championed equal protection under the law and civil rights. Ginsburg was only the second woman—and first Jewish woman—to serve on the Supreme Court.

In her new role, one of Ginsburg's best-known opinions related to gender equality was given in *United States v. Virginia* (1996), a case examining the Virginia Military Institute's male-only admissions policy. Writing for the majority of justices, she argued that state-funded institutions could not discriminate on the basis of gender. Another well-known case, for which Ginsburg wrote the

Ruth Bader Ginsburg's Collars

Ruth Bader Ginsburg was well known for her distinctive collection of jabots—large, ornamental collars—which she wore over her black Supreme Court robes. This was a tradition she started with Sandra Day O'Connor, the first woman on the Supreme Court, who served alongside Ginsburg. The standard judicial robe had been designed for men to accommodate a necktie or shirt collar underneath, so adding a jabot was a way to signify that women were now part of this traditionally male space. Many of the jabots were gifts from organizations or other nations, and Ginsburg wore them as accessories for special occasions. But in some cases she wore her collars to intentionally convey specific messages. Ginsburg's best-known jabot was her "dissent collar," which she wore whenever she was on the losing side of a Supreme Court decision vote—a bejeweled, spiky collar attached to a black band. She also had a jabot that she wore when she was part of the majority on a Supreme Court opinion, a crocheted piece made of yellow and gold fabric that somewhat resembled the sun. Other collars included a multicolored rainbow design that she wore to signify support for LGBTQ rights.

dissenting opinion, was *Ledbetter v. Goodyear Tire & Rubber Co.* (2007). In this case a longtime Goodyear employee sued because she discovered she had been paid far less than her male colleagues over the years. When the Supreme Court ruled against Ledbetter in a 5–4 decision because it said she filed her claim too late, Ginsburg implored Congress to act on this issue. In 2009 Congress passed the Lilly Ledbetter Fair Pay Act, which extended the statute of limitations for filing pay discrimination claims.

Ginsburg was also a strong supporter of reproductive rights and for upholding *Roe v. Wade*, the 1973 case that legalized abortion nationwide. She wrote the majority opinion for reproductive rights decisions in cases like *Whole Woman's Health v. Hellerstedt* (2016), which struck down a Texas law that placed stringent restrictions on abortion clinics. In 2014 she wrote the dissenting opinion to the decision of *Burwell v. Hobby Lobby Stores, Inc.*, in which the court voted 5–4 in favor of supporting Hobby Lobby's refusal to provide employee health coverage for birth control on the basis of religious beliefs.

Over the years, Ginsburg consistently took stands against laws and practices that she felt were discriminatory. She wrote opinions and dissensions for several landmark cases in support of the expansion of voting rights. In *Grutter v. Bollinger* (2003), she wrote the majority opinion in favor of affirmative action to promote diversity at colleges and universities. She was also strongly in favor of same-sex marriage, which became legal in 2015 after the case of *Obergefell v. Hodges*.

The Legacy of Ruth Bader Ginsburg

As Ginsburg aged she overcame several forms of cancer and other health problems, proudly working out daily even in her eighties. She remained on the Supreme Court until her death on September 18, 2020, from complications of pancreatic cancer. Her death was on Rosh Hashanah, one of the most significant Jewish holidays. Ginsburg's death had immediate ramifications for reproductive rights legislation. President Donald Trump replaced her on the court with conservative justice Amy Coney Barrett. This led to a conservative supermajority on the Supreme Court, which overturned *Roe v. Wade* on June 24, 2022.

However, the legacy of Ruth Bader Ginsburg's decades-long fight against gender discrimination and other forms of inequality lives on. As law professor Amanda L. Tyler writes, "Justice Ginsburg's life work was defined by her dedication to making sure the United States' Constitution leaves no one behind and truly is a document for all of us, 'We The People.'"[28]

Judy Blume, Author

In 1947, when Judy Blume was nine, her cousin got her period. Blume had no idea what this meant, so she asked her father since he was easier to talk to about personal things than her mother was. Unfortunately, her father did not explain menstruation clearly. In their awkward conversation, he said something about how periods had to do with the lunar cycle, so Blume thought women's periods were caused by the full moon. She mistakenly assumed something was wrong with her because the moon was not causing her to menstruate. "I thought, when the moon is full, every woman in the world has this wonderful thing happening to her, this menstruation thing," Blume recalled. "And I used to look out at the full moon and think, uh-uh, uh-uh. I didn't get it."[29]

Back in the 1940s—and for many years later—many young people did not have access to accurate information about menstruation, puberty, or sexuality. These topics were considered too taboo to talk about freely, so few schools taught this information, and many parents were too uncomfortable to teach their kids about them.

When Blume grew up, she had a major role in changing this. She wrote twenty-nine books, mostly for adolescents and teenagers. Blume normalized puberty and sexuality by portraying relatable protagonists who were experiencing these things. Many kids learned about periods by reading *Are You There God? It's Me, Margaret* (1970), masturbation in *Deenie* (1973), and sex and birth control in *Forever* (1975). They also read Blume's accounts of other issues that impacted their lives, like sibling rivalry, bullying, anxiety, and divorce. As journalist Rachelle Bergstein explains, "Blume offered me something no one else ever had before: a mirror of truth and a portal to some not-so-distant future, all wrapped in a humble paperback."[30]

> **"Blume offered me something no one else ever had before: a mirror of truth and a portal to some not-so-distant future, all wrapped in a humble paperback."[30]**
>
> **—Rachelle Bergstein, journalist**

Early Years

Judy Blume was born Judith Sussman in 1938 and grew up in Elizabeth, New Jersey. She described her family as a typical 1950s household that "looked good to the world."[31] Her father was a dentist, and her mother was a homemaker. Blume loved

In the twenty-nine books that Judy Blume wrote, she created relatable protagonists who were experiencing puberty and discovering sexuality.

to read, and her parents did not censor her reading list. Although she did not aspire to be a writer, she had a vivid imagination and constantly concocted stories about people in her head. "I made up stories while I bounced a ball against the side of our house," Blume says on her official website. "I made up stories playing with paper dolls. And I made them up while I practiced the piano, by pretending to give piano lessons. I even kept a notebook with the names of my pretend students and how they were doing."[32]

> **"I made up stories while I bounced a ball against the side of our house. I made up stories playing with paper dolls."[32]**
>
> **—Judy Blume**

Blume's childhood was not without hardships. When she was eight, her older brother, David, had complications after a kidney infection. With limited treatments available, Blume moved with her mother and brother to Miami Beach for two years so that he could recover in the warmer climate. Blume's father, to whom she was closest, stayed behind in New Jersey and visited them infrequently. As a young teenager, she was also traumatized after three different plane crashes in her hometown in 1951 and 1952—a memory she avoided until she wrote about the crashes in her adult novel *In the Unlikely Event* (2015).

A Turbulent Young Adulthood

Like many women in that era, Blume was expected to get married and stay home with her children. This pressure was especially strong from her mother, who gave up a career as a teacher to have a family. Although she graduated from New York University with a teaching degree, Blume saw this as a backup plan in case she ever had to work. When she was twenty-one and still in college, she married a lawyer named John Blume. He was the kind of successful "nice Jewish boy" that Blume's mother wanted her to marry. By the time she was twenty-five, she was a homemaker with two children—daughter Randy and son Larry—and lived in a four-bedroom suburban home in prestigious Scotch Plains, New Jersey. She took golf and tennis lessons.

However, Blume felt incredibly unfulfilled. Throughout her twenties she had a series of mysterious illnesses that doctors could not diagnose—which went away after she published her first novel. She divorced John in 1975, and then quickly married again. This turbulent marriage only lasted two years, and she remained single until she married a writer named George Cooper when she was forty-nine.

A Writing Career Begins

Because she felt unfulfilled, Blume decided to start writing children's stories once her kids started school. She tried for two years to publish her stories and books. Sometimes she received as many as six rejections from publishers a week—and hid in the closet to cry so her kids would not see. In 1969, when she was thirty-one, Blume published her first book—*The One in the Middle Is the Green Kangaroo*, a children's book about the difficulties of being a middle child.

To improve her craft, Blume started traveling to take a writing class at New York University, and for the first time in years, she felt like herself again and not just a wife and mother. "Monday nights were the highlight of my week because on Monday nights, I got

Starring Sally J. Freedman as Herself

Most of Judy Blume's books take place in the 1970s and 1980s, with one especially notable exception. *Starring Sally J. Freedman as Herself* (1976) is a historical novel set in 1947. Sally, the ten-year-old protagonist, is about the same age Blume was in 1947, and the book contains autobiographical parallels to Blume's childhood. Just as Blume did, Sally moves from New Jersey to Florida with her mother and brother temporarily as he recovers from a serious illness, and Sally is devastated that her father stays behind. She is terrified that he will die in a plane crash on the way to visit them. Also, like Blume, Sally is Jewish and has a vivid imagination. The book, which takes place only a few years after the Holocaust, focuses on Jewish identity more than most of Blume's other books. Haunted by the recent mass murder of Jews during the Holocaust, Sally is terrified of a neighbor because she believes he is Adolph Hitler, who she believes has secretly fled to Miami.

to take the bus into New York and go down to NYU," she writes. "And this was mine."[33]

In her writing class, Blume learned the "rules" that authors were supposed to follow when writing fiction for children and adolescents. Stories were supposed to have a clear-cut moral lesson and an ending that unambiguously reflected this message. Parents were supposed to always be right, and if children disobeyed them, they learned their lesson by the end of the book. Children could not be portrayed as defiant, especially girls. And topics like puberty and sex were forbidden. Blume did not like these rules. She preferred books like Louise Fitzhugh's groundbreaking *Harriet the Spy* (1964) and *The Long Secret* (1965), which featured defiant heroines, imperfect parents, and conversations about puberty.

Blume's first published book for adolescents was *Iggie's House* (1970), which she worked on while she was taking her writing class. *Iggie's House* is written from the perspective of eleven-year-old Winnie, who is shocked by her neighbors' racist responses when the first Black family moves into town.

Are You There, God? It's Me, Margaret

After *Iggie's House*, Blume published the book that propelled her to fame—*Are You There, God? It's Me, Margaret* (1970). The book is about Margaret Simon, an eleven-year-old girl who moves from New York City to the New Jersey suburbs. Blume says she ignored all the rules she had learned about adolescent fiction and focused on writing about "what I remember to be true about being in sixth grade."[34] Much like her protagonist Margaret, Blume had been a late bloomer, and she had conversations with God in which she begged him to let her get her period.

One way that *Are You There, God? It's Me, Margaret* broke the rules of adolescent fiction is its candid portrayal of a girl as she begins puberty. Praying she will eventually get her period, Margaret sneaks sanitary napkins (an older version of maxi pads) into her house and practices using them. In an iconic scene, Margaret and her friends perform an exercise that they hope will increase their

Blume's second published book was titled Are You There God? It's Me, Margaret. *The book was a massive success, and in 1970 the* New York Times *declared it the number one book of the year.*

breast size while chanting, "We must, we must, we must increase our bust"[35]—until one of the girls' brothers walks in and taunts them. Margaret and her friends are mean to a girl in their class who is more developed than they are, a behavior Margaret comes to regret deeply.

Book Banning Today

Judy Blume was horrified by organized efforts in the 1980s to ban books written for children and teenagers—and she is horrified today by modern efforts to keep some books out of children's hands. Today's book banning strategies tend to be more coordinated and calculated than they used to be. Nationally organized groups like Moms for Liberty and Citizens Defending Freedom put pressure on school districts to remove books throughout the country. These groups also lobby state legislatures to create stringent rules for what kinds of books can be included at libraries. Many of the books these groups object to are about LGBTQ characters, especially transgender characters. Alex Gino's *Melissa* (2015), a book about a transgender fourth grader, is one of the most targeted books. These groups also object to many books about the history of racism or novels that portray racism, like Angie Thomas's *The Hate U Give* (2017), in which a sixteen-year-old Black girl witnesses a police officer killing her friend. Groups say that books like these should be removed because they portray White characters negatively and because they are too politicized to be read in schools. Blume's books continue to be targeted for removal, especially *Forever*.

Blume also broke the rules of adolescent fiction by portraying a family that is both nontraditional and imperfect. Margaret's father was raised Jewish and her mother Christian, and Margaret was raised without religion—a situation far more controversial in 1970 than it is today. Throughout the book, Margaret explores whether she believes in God and what that means to her. The book does not downplay the family's conflict. Margaret's mother is estranged from her religious parents, and when they visit, their conflict is not resolved happily. The grandparents push their beliefs on Margaret, who defiantly argues with them, and they leave.

Blume's book was a massive success. In 1970 the *New York Times* declared it to be the number one book of the year. The book spoke to girls who had never read anything so candid about their real-life experiences. "We . . . had so many questions, ones we barely had the language to articulate and only dared to whisper in the dark during a sleepover," explains *New York Times* book reviewer Elisabeth Egan. "Margaret asked these questions, and

Blume answered with candor and respect."[36] In 2023 the book was made into a movie.

Groundbreaking Books

Throughout the 1970s and 1980s, Blume continued to write books about topics that resonated with young people. In *It's Not the End of the World* (1972), twelve-year-old Karen navigates her parents' divorce—a common issue for kids growing up at the time. In *Blubber* (1974), fifth grader Jill is part of a group of girls who bully an overweight classmate, until Jill's so-called friends start bullying her instead. *Tiger Eyes* (1981), one of Blume's darkest books, follows fifteen-year-old Davey as she copes with her father's violent death.

Blume also wrote books from the perspective of boys. *Then Again, Maybe I Won't* (1971) deals with puberty, anxiety, and family problems from the perspective of twelve-year-old Tony, who uses binoculars to spy on the girl next door. Blume also wrote *Tales of a Fourth Grade Nothing* (1972) and its three sequels about Peter, a boy who feels overshadowed by his mischievous younger brother Fudge—who, among other things, swallows Peter's beloved turtle.

Blume's most controversial book was *Forever* (1975), a love story about high school senior Katherine and her boyfriend, Michael, who have a sexual relationship. *Forever* was inspired in part by a conversation Blume had with her teenage daughter, who was frustrated that anytime she read books in which teenagers have sex, the characters died or were otherwise punished for their actions. *Forever* does not do this, and it explicitly portrays the emotional and sexual elements of Katherine and Michael's relationship. The book includes a scene in which Katherine goes to a clinic to get birth control pills, where she (and the reader) learns more about pregnancy prevention.

Censorship

Not everyone appreciated Blume's candid books. She first encountered censorship of her books after she published *Are You There, God? It's Me, Margaret*. She donated three copies of the book to her children's elementary school library. The principal angrily removed the books from the shelves. He did not think it was appropriate for elementary school students to read about menstruation, even though some of them were old enough to have their periods.

In the 1980s, as the country took a conservative turn, campaigns to censor books by authors like Judy Blume intensified. Protestors handed out pamphlets at malls and supermarkets about how to pressure libraries to get rid of Judy Blume's books. Blume, who never intentionally set out to write controversial materials, was shocked. "Book banning satisfies their need to feel in control of their children's lives," she explains. "This fear is often disguised as moral outrage. They want to believe that if their children don't read about it, their children won't know about it. And if they don't know about it, it won't happen."[37]

As a result, Blume became an outspoken anti-censorship activist. In the 1980s she became a board member of the Na-

Judy Blume and her husband, George Cooper, in their bookstore in Key West, Florida.

tional Coalition Against Censorship, and over the years she has given hundreds of talks and interviews about the dangers of banning books. She has frequently argued that books about controversial topics are essential because they help young people cope with difficult situations. In 1999 she published an anthology of original stories written by children's book authors who had been censored, called *Places I Never Meant to Be: Original Stories by Censored Writers*.

> **"Where stammering parents and mortified health teachers fumbled, Blume provided simple language for embarrassing and awkward conversations."[38]**
>
> —Elisabeth Egan, *New York Times* book reviewer

Judy Blume's Legacy

Judy Blume's books have sold over 90 million copies worldwide. Her realistic portrayals of young people have transformed the norms of writing books for children and adolescents. "Where stammering parents and mortified health teachers fumbled, Blume provided simple language for embarrassing and awkward conversations," writes Egan. "She elevated honesty to an art form."[38] As of 2024, Blume lived in Key West, Florida, with her husband, where they ran a bookstore.

Mayim Bialik, Actor and Neuroscientist

On *The Big Bang Theory* (2007–2019), one of the most popular sitcoms of all time, actor Mayim Bialik played the role of a neuroscientist named Dr. Amy Farrah Fowler. During the 2019 series finale, Dr. Fowler and her husband, Sheldon Cooper, won the Nobel Prize for their joint research. In her acceptance speech, Dr. Fowler spoke to girls. "I would just like to take this moment to say to all the young girls out there who dream about science as a profession to go for it," she said. "It is the greatest job in the world. If anyone tells you you can't, don't listen."[39]

Dr. Fowler's speech was especially powerful because of the similarities between Mayim Bialik and the character she played on TV. Like Amy Farrah Fowler, Bialik also has a PhD in neuroscience, and she has been an outspoken advocate of girls pursuing STEM careers. The speech given by Dr. Fowler could have easily been written by Bialik.

Bialik may be the only woman in history who is both a neuroscientist and an actor who played one on a sitcom. Her career path from child actor to neuroscientist and then back to acting has been unique, especially combined with all the other professional and personal roles she has played. Bialik is also a podcaster, an author, a blogger, and a very devoted mother of two boys. She also is an observant Modern Orthodox Jew.

Early Life

Mayim Bialik was born in San Diego, California, in 1975. Her uncommon first name means "water" in Hebrew. Three of Bialik's four grandparents were immigrants from eastern Europe who fled to the United States because of rising violence against Jews in the 1920s and 1930s.

After growing up in traditionally observant Jewish homes, Mayim's parents, Barry and Beverly, opted to raise Bialik and her brother as Reform Jews. They were not very religious. However, her childhood home was filled with Jewish artifacts that her grandparents had brought from the old country—like a needlepoint her grandmother had made of the Western Wall, a holy Jewish site in Jerusalem. Yiddish, the language spoken by Bialik's grandparents and other Jews in eastern Europe, was often spoken at home. Her family celebrated Jewish holidays like Passover and Hanukkah with an emphasis on making them fun.

Bialik's parents were both English teachers and documentary filmmakers. Growing up as a second-generation American in an intellectual family, Bialik often felt like she was different from other kids even before she became famous. Bialik described her family life as loving but dysfunctional. "I grew up in a complicated home," she writes. "It was a loving, hilarious, artistically inspiring, and supportive home, but my parents struggled with mental illness. . . .

Mayim Bialik, in a scene from the sitcom The Big Bang Theory, *appears with the character Sheldon Cooper.*

Many of my decisions about how I lead my life stem from the tools I had to acquire in order to cope in a home that was riddled with mental health disorders."[40]

Despite these challenges, Bialik's parents were supportive. When Bialik started acting in elementary school plays, they encouraged her to pursue acting professionally. When she was eleven, Bialik started auditioning weekly for television and movie roles.

A Childhood Acting Career

Breaking into Hollywood as a child actor is a dream that few people realize. Bialik's rapid rise to success was unlikely, especially because her quirky personality and appearance did not conform to traditional Hollywood standards. She was aware of how different she was from other girls in Hollywood. "I was expected to look a certain way and act a certain way—all while going from being a girl to a young woman in front of everyone's eyes," she writes. "It was a lot of pressure."[41] Bialik coped with the help of her mother, who encouraged her to be herself.

> **"I was expected to look a certain way and act a certain way—all while going from being a girl to a young woman in front of everyone's eyes."[41]**
>
> **—Mayim Bialik**

When she was twelve, Bialik was cast in her first role: a small part in the horror movie *Pumpkinhead* (1988). She also landed guest roles on popular sitcoms like *The Facts of Life* and *Webster*. Then she was cast in her breakout role in *Beaches* (1988), a very successful movie about the lifelong friendship of two women. One of the women was played by Bette Midler—a prominent Jewish actor—and Bialik played the role of Midler's character as a child. The producers cast her because she captured the sassy personality of Midler's character.

When Bialik was fifteen, she was cast as the lead on the NBC sitcom *Blossom*, which aired from 1991 to 1995. Bialik played Blossom Russo, an eccentric teenager who lives with her single father and two brothers. The show was praised for its realistic portrayal of a teenage girl, and Blossom often broke the fourth

At age fifteen, Bialik was cast as the lead character in the NBC sitcom Blossom.

wall by talking directly to the audience about her insights and feelings. "*Blossom* was kind of ahead of its time in a lot of ways," explains Bialik. "To have a show about a girl on network television at that time was super unusual. No one thought it would work."[42]

Switching to Science

When *Blossom* ended, Bialik put acting aside to go to college. As the child of two teachers, she valued education as much as they did—and on top of that, she was tired of being part of an industry that objectified women and girls. "I craved being around people who valued me more for what was inside my brain than what was inside my bra,"[43] she writes.

Bialik wanted to study science. Her interest in science had been sparked by a tutor she worked with while she was on *Blossom*. She explains:

> I had a tutor who was the first female role model I ever had who showed me that someone could be as passionate about biology as I thought you could only be about art or poetry. She was young and hip and made the sciences come alive, and it was she that inspired me and really gave me the confidence and the skill-set to go on to a bachelor's degree and eventually a Ph.D. in neuroscience.[44]

After high school, Bialik was accepted to both Harvard and Yale, but instead she decided to attend the University of California, Los Angeles (UCLA). She wanted to be close to her family. Bialik had a great experience at UCLA, where she got to know people from different cultures and socioeconomic backgrounds—something that was missing from her experience as a Hollywood actress. She majored in neuroscience and minored in both Hebrew and Jew-

What Is Neuroscience?

Mayim Bialik's field of study, neuroscience, is the study of the nervous system, including the brain, spinal cord, and all the body's nerves. This is an exciting field of study because over the past fifty years, new technology has made it possible to study the brain in ways that were not possible before. Neuroscientists study how the brain works and how it influences behavior, emotions, thoughts, memories, and all other cognitive processes. They study how different parts of the nervous system communicate with each other and how breakdowns in that communication system can contribute to Alzheimer's disease, epilepsy, and mental health conditions like depression. Research in neuroscience helps doctors treat brain injuries, dementia, and mental illnesses. Other neuroscience research has led to greater understanding and treatment options for people with neurodivergent conditions like autism and attention-deficit/hyperactivity disorder. Advances in imaging tools, such as magnetic resonance imaging and other brain-scanning technologies, have allowed scientists to observe brain activity in real time and uncover the complex ways our brains work. "I love understanding the way we think and feel and communicate—and neuroscience is the science of all that," explains Bialik.

Quoted in Abby Ellin, "How Actress Mayim Bialik Encourages Girls to Love Science," *Brain and Life*, October/November 2018. www.brainandlife.org.

> "I had a tutor who was the first female role model I ever had who showed me that someone could be as passionate about biology as I thought you could only be about art or poetry."[44]
>
> —Mayim Bialik

ish studies. After graduating, she continued her studies at UCLA with the goal of becoming a research scientist. In 2007 she completed a PhD in neuroscience, writing a dissertation about the relationship between two brain chemicals and obsessive-compulsive disorder in teenagers who have a genetic condition called Prader-Willi syndrome.

Jewish Identity

During the years she was in school, Bialik explored her Jewish identity. Although she was raised in a mostly secular household, Bialik was drawn at an early age to practicing Judaism in a more traditionally religious way. She was the first woman in her family to have a bat mitzvah—a coming-of-age ceremony for Jewish girls at which they recite a passage from the Torah—and she described the experience as spiritually profound. She also experimented with keeping kosher as a teenager. In college Bialik was heavily involved with the campus Hillel, a Jewish student organization. She studied Judaism alongside her then-fiancé Michael Stone, who converted to Judaism before they married, and has continued to work with religious study partners over the years.

Bialik now identifies as Modern Orthodox, which means she practices a form of Judaism that upholds traditional Jewish law and customs while engaging with the modern world. As part of her practice of Judaism, Bialik chooses to dress modestly and almost never wears pants.

An Acting Career Restarts with a Bang

In the late 2000s, Bialik decided to step away from research and go back to acting. Although she loved science, she missed performing and felt that acting would allow her to have more time with her children Miles (born in 2005) and Frederick (born in 2008). Now in her thirties, Bialik did not expect to land major roles. "As a 'nontraditional'-looking woman, I came back to an industry that had me auditioning for the 'frumpy friend' or the 'zaftig secretary,'"[45] she explains. She was cast in minor recurring roles on HBO's *Curb Your Enthusiasm* and ABC Family's *The Secret Life of the American Teenager*.

Then in 2010, Bialik was cast on what was originally supposed to be a single episode of *The Big Bang Theory*. Despite the show's popularity, Bialik had never seen it. "I thought it was a game show,"[46] she recalls. Bialik was introduced as Amy Farrah Fowler, a potential love interest and the female equivalent of socially inept genius Sheldon Cooper. The role was such a hit that she was asked to come back for several additional episodes, and after eight episodes, she was added to the cast. Amy became a part of the core group of friends on the show and eventually married Sheldon.

> **"I am grateful to bring Amy Farrah Fowler to life on the No. 1 sitcom in America. I am honored to depict a feminist who speaks her mind, who loves science and her friends and who sometimes wishes she were the hot girl."[47]**
>
> **—Mayim Bialik**

Playing Amy was an unexpected and remarkable opportunity for Bialik. For one thing, she and Amy were strikingly similar. Amy was a neuroscientist who dressed modestly, and Bialik could relate to her social awkwardness, which was kind of an exaggerated version of her own. Bialik also valued playing Amy because she was such an unconventional sitcom character. Unlike the simplistic portrayal of many young single women in sitcoms, Amy was a complex character who defied expectations of how a woman should look and act. "I am grateful to bring Amy Farrah Fowler to life on the No. 1 sitcom in America," she wrote in 2017. "I am honored to depict a feminist who speaks her mind, who loves science and her friends and who sometimes wishes she were the hot girl."[47] In Bialik's nine seasons on the show, she was nominated four times for an Emmy Award in the category of Outstanding Supporting Actress in a Comedy Series.

Bialik continued to act after *The Big Bang Theory* ended in 2019. From 2021 to 2023, she starred as the lead in the Fox sitcom *Call Me Kat*, in which she played an unconventional woman who opens a cat café. During this time, she also was one of the hosts (along with Ken Jennings) of the game show *Jeopardy!* As of 2024 Bialik was working with Don Reo, the former producer of *Blossom*, on a possible *Blossom* reboot.

A Multifaceted Career

As if being both an actor and a scientist were not enough, Bialik has quite a few other accomplishments. She has written four books, including a vegan cookbook and a parenting book. In collaboration with DC Comics, Bialik also edited a 2021 graphic novel anthology featuring stories meant to excite kids about STEM topics. Since 2010 she has written a blog for Kveller, a Jewish parenting website, where she also created six lighthearted information videos about Jewish holidays. From 2015 to 2019, she also had her own website, Grok Nation, where she wrote about everything from popular culture to political activism to her own experiences.

Bialik is also a podcaster. Since 2021 she and her romantic partner, Jonathan Cohen, have hosted the podcast *Mayim Bialik's*

In addition to being an accomplished actor and scientist, Mayim Bialik is the author of several books, including the parenting book titled Beyond the Sling.

Supporting STEM Education

In addition to Mayim Bialik's work as an actor and scientist, she has been an outspoken advocate for encouraging young people—especially girls—to consider studying fields in science, technology, engineering, and mathematics, or STEM. As a college student, it always bothered Bialik to see how uncommon it was for women to major in many STEM fields, especially computer science and physics. "I'm using my visibility to encourage girls and young women to take an interest in science and give them a deeper understanding of what they can do in that world," she says. In 2013 Bialik became a spokesperson for DeVry University's HerWorld initiative, a program designed to get high school girls excited about STEM fields and to encourage them to pursue careers in STEM. In addition, she also taught classes for homeschooled high school students in her home about biology, chemistry, and neuroscience.

Quoted in Abby Ellin, "How Actress Mayim Bialik Encourages Girls to Love Science," *Brain and Life*, October/November 2018. www.brainandlife.org.

Breakdown, which focuses on mental health issues. The podcast regularly features psychologists, neuroscientists, and other experts, as well as celebrities talking candidly about their own mental health issues. Inspired by Bialik's own mental health struggles and the struggles her parents had when she was growing up, the goal of the podcast is to make mental health issues engaging and accessible.

As an actor, scientist, parent, observant Jew, and so much more, Mayim Bialik demonstrates that people can be complicated and defy easy definitions—and that this is a good thing. She writes:

> I'm a girl who didn't always fit in. I'm the girl who loved science but didn't know how to pursue it; I'm a creative person who loves the arts but also embraces a scientific perspective on life; and I am an independent woman who also loves being a mom. I've spent so much of my life challenging myself to be more and do more than I thought I could be, and it's paid off with a hectic and sometimes challenging life, but it's also a life I am proud of.[48]

SOURCE NOTES

Introduction: The Contributions of American Jewish Women

1. Sasha Lasakow, "Dignity and Strength: Celebrating Jewish Women," *Temple News*, November 7, 2017. https://temple-news.com.
2. Joyce Antler, "The History of Jewish Women in the United States," *Oxford Research Encyclopedia*, May 24, 2023. https://oxfordre.com.
3. Hasia R. Diner, ed., *Doing Business in America: A Jewish History*. West Lafayette, IN: Purdue University Press, 2018, p. ix.

Chapter One: Ida Cohen Rosenthal, Businesswoman

4. Sierra B. Holt, "Why Fight Nature? A Biography of the Early Life of Ida Rosenthal," master's thesis, City University of New York, 2021, p. 6. https://academicworks.cuny.edu.
5. Joy A. Kingsolver, "Ida Cohen Rosenthal," Jewish Women's Archive, March 20, 2009. https://jwa.org.
6. Quoted in Jewish Women's Archive, "Power Couples: Undergarment Entrepreneurs." https://jwa.org.
7. Quoted in Natasha Synycia, "Ida Rosenthal and Her Maidenformidable Empire: Booming Business and Dreamy Advertising in Postwar United States," doctoral dissertation, University of California, Irvine, 2016, p. 29. https://escholarship.org.
8. Quoted in *New York Times*, "Ida Rosenthal, Co-founder of Maidenform Dies," March 30, 1973. www.nytimes.com.
9. Holt, "Why Fight Nature?," p. 16.

Chapter Two: Gertrude Elion, Biochemist and Pharmacologist

10. Quoted in Catherine Whitlock and Rhodri Evans, *10 Women Who Changed Science and the World*. New York: Diversion, 2019, p. 85.
11. Nobel Prize, "Gertrude B. Elion." www.nobelprize.org.
12. Quoted in Nobel Prize, "Gertrude B. Elion."
13. Quoted in Luca Nicola, "Gertrude: The Scientist Who Revolutionized Pharmacology," IBSA Foundation for Scientific Research, November 11, 2020. www.ibsafoundation.org.
14. Quoted in Sharon Bertsch McGrayne, "Damn the Torpedoes! Full Speed Ahead," *Science*, May 3, 2002, p. 852. www.science.org.

15. Quoted in Whitlock and Evans, *10 Women Who Changed Science and the World*, pp. 94–95.
16. Nobel Prize, "Gertrude B. Elion."
17. Quoted in Zing Tsjeng, *Forgotten Women: The Scientists*. London: Hachette, 2018, p. 98.
18. Quoted in Nobel Prize, "Gertrude B. Elion."
19. Quoted in Whitlock and Evans, *10 Women Who Changed Science and the World*, p. 108.

Chapter Three: Ruth Bader Ginsburg, Supreme Court Justice

20. Quoted in CBS News, "How Ruth Bader Ginsburg Became a 'Notorious' Cultural Icon," September 21, 2020. www.cbsnews.com.
21. Quoted in Amy Laskowski, "'RBG Convinced Me I Could Make a Difference in the World,'" BU Today, September 22, 2020. www.bu.edu.
22. Quoted in Geoff Blackwell, *Ruth Bader Ginsburg: I Know This to Be True*. San Francisco, CA: Chronicle, 2020, p. 11.
23. Quoted in Yonat Shimron, "Ruth Bader Ginsburg Was Passionate About Judaism's Concern for Justice," *Washington Post*, September 18, 2020. www.washingtonpost.com.
24. Quoted in Samara Stone, "Unpacking Ruth Bader Ginsburg's Jewish Roots," Unpacked, March 4, 2024. https://jewishunpacked.com.
25. Quoted in Linda Greenhouse, "Ruth Bader Ginsburg, Supreme Court's Feminist Icon, Is Dead at 87," *New York Times*, September 18, 2020. www.nytimes.com.
26. Quoted in Liz Mineo, "The Life and Legacy of RBG," *Harvard Gazette*, September 2020. https://news.harvard.edu.
27. Quoted in Blackwell, *Ruth Bader Ginsburg*, pp. 14–15.
28. Ruth Bader Ginsburg and Amanda L. Tyler, *Justice, Justice, Thou Shalt Pursue*. Oakland: University of California Press, 2021, p. 264.

Chapter Four: Judy Blume, Author

29. Quoted in Life Stories, *Judy Blume Interview: On Her Writing Career & Fighting Against Censorship*, YouTube, April 21, 2023. www.youtube.com/watch?v=2xEP6RFXwqQ.
30. Rachelle Bergstein, *The Genius of Judy: How Judy Blume Rewrote Childhood for All of Us*. New York: Atria/One Signal, 2024, p. xvi.
31. Quoted in Life Stories, *Judy Blume Interview*.
32. Judy Blume, "How I Became an Author," Judy Blume on the Web. https://judyblume.com.
33. Quoted in Life Stories, *Judy Blume Interview*.

34. Quoted in Life Stories, *Judy Blume Interview*.
35. Quoted in Life Stories, *Judy Blume Interview*.
36. Elisabeth Egan, "Why *Are You There God? It's Me, Margaret* Still Matters," *New York Times*, April 27, 2023. www.nytimes.com.
37. Judy Blume, "Judy Blume Talks About Censorship," Judy Blume on the Web. https://judyblume.com.
38. Elisabeth Egan, "The Essential Judy Blume," *New York Times*, September 14, 2022. www.nytimes.com.

Chapter Five: Mayim Bialik, Actor and Neuroscientist

39. Quoted in Mark Cendrowski, director, *The Big Bang Theory*, Season 12, episode 24, "The Stockholm Syndrome," aired May 16, 2019, on CBS.
40. Mayim Bialik, "Memories of John Lennon Helped Me Tell the Story of My Jewish Family," Kveller, February 3, 2021. www.kveller.com.
41. Mayim Bialik, *Girling Up: How to Be Strong, Smart, and Spectacular*. New York: Philomel, 2017, p. 3.
42. Quoted in Yahoo! Entertainment, *Mayim Bialik Reflects on* Blossom, Beaches*, and Why She Didn't Feel "Normal" Growing Up*, YouTube, June 10, 2021. www.youtube.com/watch?v=ob_94PSYfaA.
43. Mayim Bialik, "Being a Feminist in Harvey Weinstein's World," *New York Times*, October 13, 2017. www.nytimes.com.
44. Quoted in Meghan Casserly, "Mayim Bialik's *Big Bang Theory* on Girls, STEM Careers and Role Models," *Forbes*, March 15, 2013. www.forbes.com.
45. Bialik, "Being a Feminist in Harvey Weinstein's World."
46. Quoted in CBS News, "'I Thought *The Big Bang Theory* Was a Game Show': Mayim Bialik on Playing Amy Farrah Fowler," April 9, 2021. www.cbsnews.com.
47. Bialik, "Being a Feminist in Harvey Weinstein's World."
48. Bialik, *Girling Up*, p. 4.

Books

Rachelle Bergstein, *The Genius of Judy: How Judy Blume Rewrote Childhood for All of Us*. New York: Atria/One Signal, 2024.

Mayim Bialik, *Girling Up: How to Be Strong, Smart, and Spectacular*. New York: Philomel, 2017.

Jane Sherron De Hart, *Ruth Bader Ginsburg: A Life*. New York: Knopf Doubleday, 2020.

Nadine Epstein, *RBG's Brave and Brilliant Women: 33 Jewish Women to Inspire Everyone*. New York: Delacorte, 2021.

Ruth Bader Ginsburg and Amanda L. Tyler, *Justice, Justice, Thou Shalt Pursue: My Life's Work Fighting for a More Perfect Union*. New York: Simon & Schuster, 2023.

Pamela S. Nadel, *America's Jewish Women: A History from Colonial Times to Today*. New York: Norton, 2019.

Catherine Whitlock and Rhodri Evans, *10 Women Who Changed Science and the World*. New York: Diversion, 2019.

Internet Sources

Patrick Adams, "Meet the Woman Who Gave the World Antiviral Drugs," *National Geographic*, August 31, 2020. www.nationalgeographic.com.

Joyce Antler, "The History of Jewish Women in the United States," *Oxford Research Encyclopedia*, May 24, 2023. https://oxfordre.com.

Michelle Byers, "Mayim Bialik," Jewish Women's Archive, June 23, 2021. https://jwa.org.

Joy A. Kingsolver, "Ida Cohen Rosenthal," Jewish Women's Archive, March 20, 2009. https://jwa.org.

Life Stories, *Judy Blume Interview: On Her Writing Career & Fighting Against Censorship*, YouTube, April 21, 2023. www.youtube.com/watch?v=2xEP6RFXwqQ.

Unpacked Staff, "Inspiring Jewish Women You Should Know About," Unpacked, March 8, 2022. https://jewishunpacked.com.

Websites

Grok Nation

https://groknation.com
Grok Nation was Mayim Bialik's personal website that was active from 2015 to 2019 but is still available to read. The site includes Bialik's insights into her personal experiences as well as commentary on current events, popular culture, and Jewish topics.

Jewish Biographies: Women, Jewish Virtual Library

www.jewishvirtuallibrary.org/jewish-women-biographies
This collection includes hundreds of short biographical entries about prominent Jewish women around the world.

Jewish Women's Archive

https://jwa.org
This website provides a comprehensive collection of articles, interviews, and other information about Jewish women in America, including profiles of notable Jewish women. The site also contains reflections by young women on what it means to them to be Jewish.

Judy Blume on the Web

https://judyblume.com
This is the official website of author Judy Blume. It includes information about her life, her books, censorship, and writing.

INDEX

Note: Boldface page numbers indicate illustrations.

PICTURE CREDITS

Cover: Dfree:Shutterstock

6: Piero Oliosi/Polaris/Newscom
9: adsR/Alamy Stock Photo
15: Associated Press
20: Pictorial Press Ltd/Alamy Stock Photo
22: Cardirin/Shutterstock
26: Associated Press
29: Ira Berger/Alamy Stock Photo
31: Associated Press
35: The Syndicate/Alamy Stock Photo
39: Associated Press
43: Sam Oaksey/Alamy Stock Photo
46: Associated Press
49: TCD/Prod.DB/Alamy Stock Photo
51: Album/Alamy Stock Photo
55: MediaPunch Inc/Alamy Stock Photo

ABOUT THE AUTHOR

Naomi Rockler is an educational freelance writer who writes nonfiction and fiction books for teenagers. She lives in Minnesota with her husband and daughter.